Contents

Introduction to English   page 2

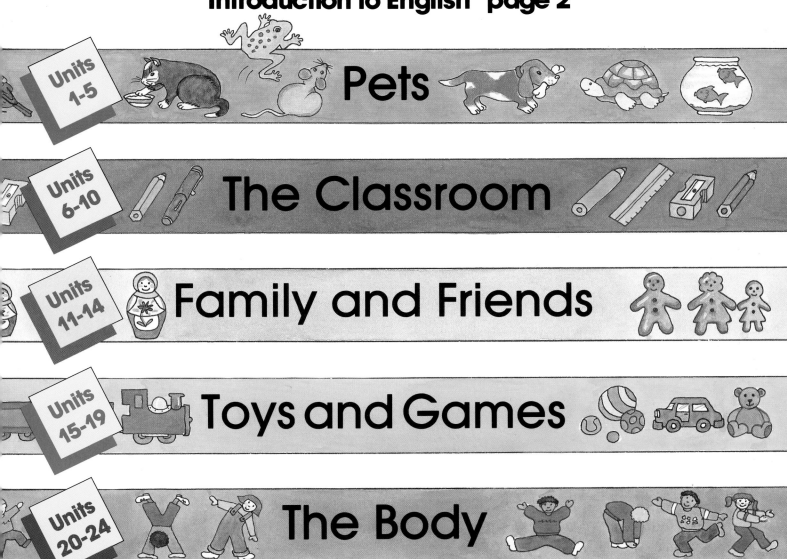

SONG — COLOURS

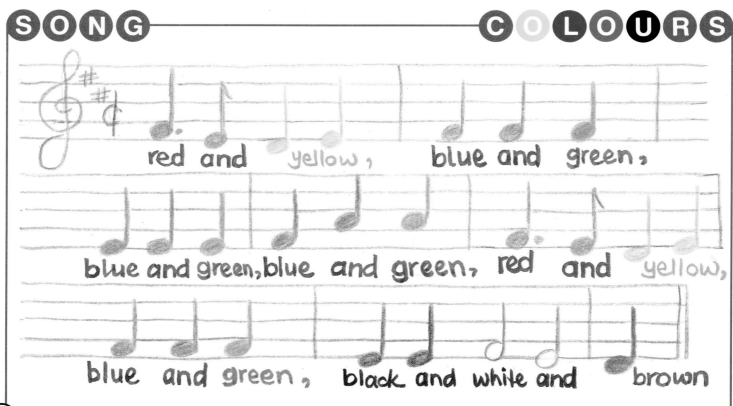

red and yellow, blue and green,

blue and green, blue and green, red and yellow,

blue and green, black and white and brown

You need: × 7

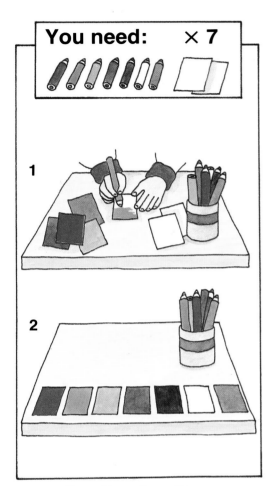

1

2

🎞 What number?

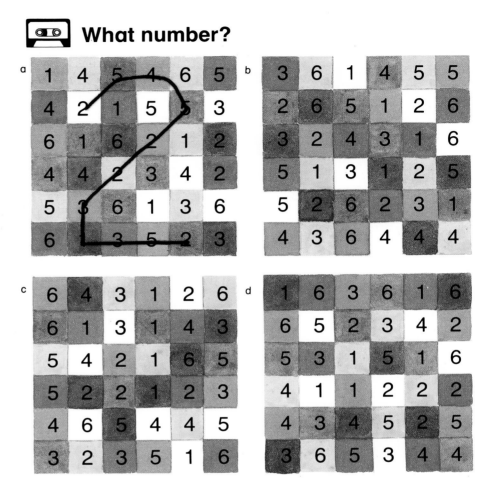

a
1	4	5	4	6	5
4	2	1	5	5	3
6	1	6	2	1	2
4	4	2	3	4	2
5	3	6	1	3	6
6	1	3	5	2	3

b
3	6	1	4	5	5
2	6	5	1	2	6
3	2	4	3	1	6
5	1	3	1	2	5
5	2	6	2	3	1
4	3	6	4	4	4

c
6	4	3	1	2	6
6	1	3	1	4	3
5	4	2	1	6	5
5	2	2	1	2	3
4	6	5	4	4	5
3	2	3	5	1	6

d
1	6	3	6	1	6
6	5	2	3	4	2
5	3	1	5	1	6
4	1	1	2	2	2
4	3	4	5	2	5
3	6	5	3	4	4

R H Y M E

One potato . . .

One potato, two potatoes, three potatoes, four,
five potatoes, six potatoes, seven potatoes,

MORE!

1

Pets

Kate's Snake

Who's this?   Julie.

Who's this?   Butch.

Who's this?   Kate.

Who's this?   Sam.

Who's this?   Kev.

Hello! I'm Kate. What's your name?

Hi! I'm Julie. What's your name?

Bill's Tortoise

Who's this?	Who's this?	Who's this?	Who's this?	Who's this?
Suzy.	Duffy.	Bill.	Wow.	Slow.

B I N G O
B I N G O
B I N G O

STOP!
green and brown
white
black and white
red and yellow
brown

What's this?	A dog.
What's this?	A cat.
What's this?	A mouse.
What's this?	A tortoise.
What's this?	A snake.

Is this <u>Kev</u>?

Yes.

1

2

3

4

5

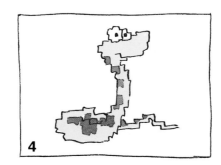

Suzy's Drawings

Ha, ha! Is this a dog?

No, it's a cat!

Is this a monkey?

No, it's you!

Is this a boy?	Is this Kate?	Is this a snake?
No, it's a girl.	No, it's Kev.	No, it's a tortoise.

1

This is Kate's snake. His name is Sam.
He's red and yellow.

2

This is Suzy's cat. Her name is Duffy.
She's black and white.

SONG Old MacDonald

Old MacDonald had a farm,
E-1-E-1-O
And on that farm he had a dog,
E-1-E-1-O
With a woof woof here and a woof woof there
Here a woof, there a woof,
Everywhere a woof,
Old MacDonald had a farm,
E-1-E-1-O.

Our Pets

I'm Kev. My mouse is called Wow.

This is Bill. His tortoise is called Slow.

This is Julie. Her dog is called Butch.

STEPPING STONES GAME

Make a snake   You need:

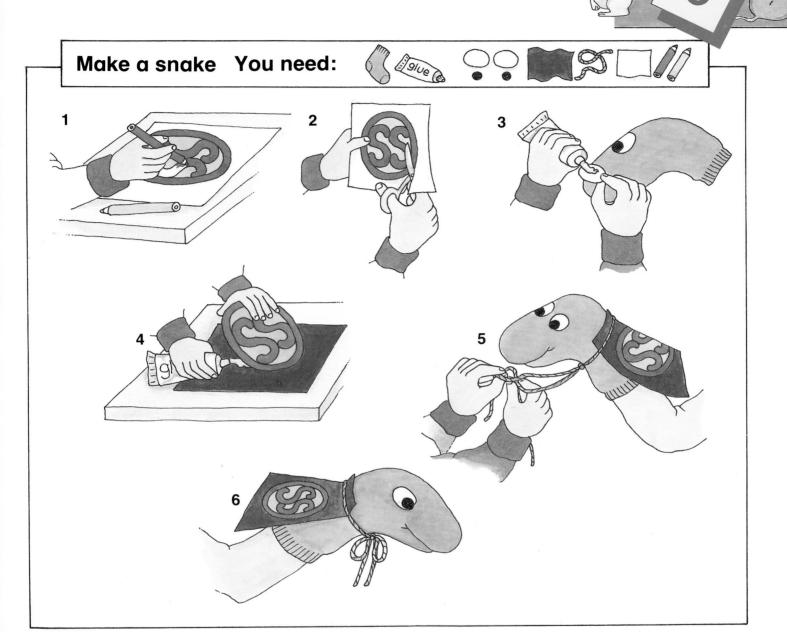

Where's Wow?

What's this? | **A <u>bag</u>.** | **Is this a <u>book</u>?** | **No, it's a <u>bag</u>.**

a bag **a pencil** **a book** **a chair** **a table**

SONG — COLOURS

orange, purple, pink and grey

pink and grey pink and grey orange, purple,

pink and grey black and white and brown

Make a Spinning Top **You need:** card colours scissors pencil ruler

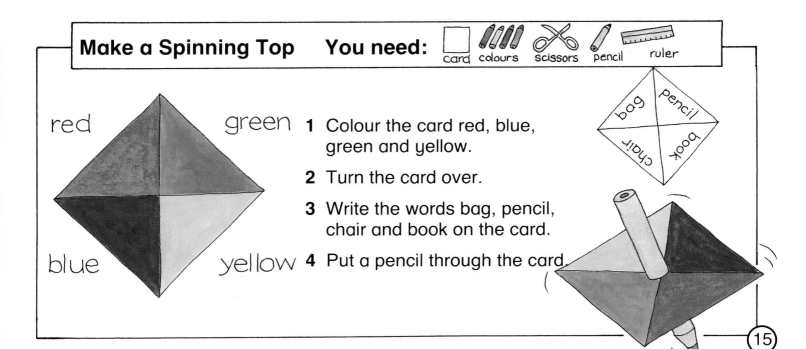

red   green

1 Colour the card red, blue, green and yellow.

2 Turn the card over.

3 Write the words bag, pencil, chair and book on the card.

blue   yellow   4 Put a pencil through the card.

What is it?

What's this? A pen. **What colour's the pen?** Blue.

 a pen

 a rubber

 a ruler

 a pencil sharpener

 a pencil case

*What's number 1?
I don't know.
Is it a door?
Oh, yes!*

 1
 2
 3
 4
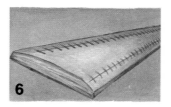 5
 6
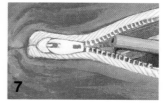 7

16

Can I borrow . . ?

Can I borrow your pen?   No, not your pencil, your pen.

 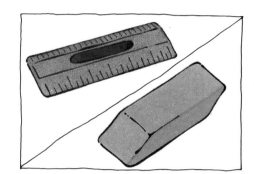 

SONG

Ten Little Indians

1 little, 2 little, 3 little Indians.
4 little, 5 little, 6 little Indians.
7 little, 8 little, 9 little Indians.
10 little Indian boys.

10 little, 9 little, 8 little Indians.
7 little, 6 little, 5 little Indians.
4 little, 3 little, 2 little Indians.
1 little Indian boy.

Where's the rubber?

I don't know.

Well, guess!

No, wrong!

Er.. there!

O.K, there!

Right!

Where's the bag?

On the table.

Where's the pen?

In the box.

Where's the rubber?

Under the table.

Where's the ruler?

In the bag.

Is this your mouse?

STEPPING STONES GAME

This is Bill's teacher.
Her name is Mrs King.

This is Suzy's teacher.
His name is Mr Bell.

10

1 one   6 six
2 two   7 seven
3 three   8 eight
4 four   9 nine
5 five   10 ten

How many pencils?

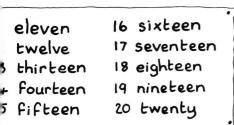

eleven	16	sixteen
twelve	17	seventeen
thirteen	18	eighteen
fourteen	19	nineteen
fifteen	20	twenty

What colour's the **book**?

SUPERSNAKE

This is the worm school.

SCHOOL

The worms are in the classroom.

4+5 =
3+2 =
2+4 =

Maths
1+1 = 2
2+1 = 5,
4+5 =

Oh, dear! What is four and five?

Willy, what's four and five?

That's very difficult. I don't know.

Hey, look! There's Supersnake!

Look. A number!

It's number nine.

Four and five is nine.

Maths
1+1 = 2
2+1 = 5,
4+5 =

Thanks, Supersnake. Goodbye.

Family Photographs

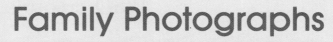

These are his photographs

His grandfather and grandmother

His father and mother

And his brothers and sisters. He's got 21 brothers and 19 sisters.

This is my family.
I've got one brother and
one sister. My brother
is called Gary and my
sister is called Suzy. My
father and mother are
called Mr and Mrs Kay.
My grandfather and
grandmother are called
Mr and Mrs Mills.

Who's this?

Me

my brother

my sister

my father

my mother

my grandfather

my grandmother

My Friend

This is my friend Kev.

Hello, Kev. How are you?

Fine, thanks.

Hi, mum. Where's Duffy?

Here! She's on the table.

Oh, dear! Duffy isn't Wow's friend.

Who's Kev?

Bill's friend.

Who's Gary?

Suzy's brother.

SUPERSNAKE

Willy, these are my friends. Sid snail and Cathy caterpillar.

Hello.

Hello.

Hi.

Is that your friend Supersnake?

No, it isn't. It's a bird. Quick, everybody. Let's go!

Where are they?

I'm in here.

We're under the ground.

13 Happy Birthday

SONG

I'm Kate. I'm seven years old. My friend Suzy is eight years old. Her little brother Gary is five.

How old is Kate?	Seven.
What's her friend called?	Suzy.
How old is she?	Eight.
What's her little brother called?	Gary.
How old is he?	Five.

28

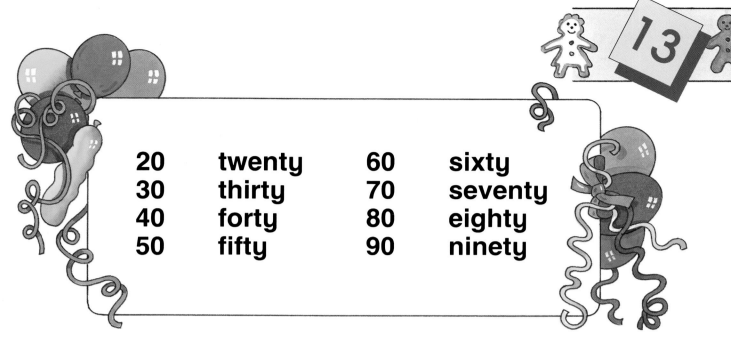

20	twenty	60	sixty
30	thirty	70	seventy
40	forty	80	eighty
50	fifty	90	ninety

 **How many <u>children</u> are there?**

children

cards

badges

candles

My Family

I'm Bill Kay. I've got one brother and one sister. My sister's name is Suzy. She's eight years old. My brother's name is Gary. He's five years old.

I'm Suzy Kay. I've got two brothers. Their names are Bill and Gary. Bill is nine and Gary is five.

SUPERSNAKE

What's that?

A card. It's Supersnake's birthday.

How old is he?

I don't know.

Oh, dear! I haven't got a card for Supersnake.

I know...

HAPPY BIRTHDAY

QUIZ

What colour is Supersnake?

What is Bill's father's name?

How old is Slow?

What is Suzy's teacher called?

What colour is Cathy Caterpillar?

How old is Gary's mother?

How many brothers and sisters has Wow got?

How many children are there in Bill's family?

Is Duffy a dog?

Name two of Willy Worm's friends.

What colour is Kev's mouse?

How many brothers has Kate got?

Who is Bill's tortoise?

Is Mr Kay Bill's father or his grandfather?

What is Julie's dog called?

How old is Bill?

Who is Kev's sister?

Name Suzy's brothers.

Who is Bill's grandmother?

What is seventeen and twenty two?

There are toys everywhere!

Kev and Kate are in their bedroom. They are playing with their toys. Kev is playing with his trains and Kate is playing with her cars.
There are toys everywhere. There are two dolls and a kite in the toy box. And there are two balls on the floor by the toy box.
There is a robot on the bed and a blue car under the bed. There are two teddies and a ball by the bed. The big teddy is orange and the little teddy is brown.

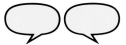

What's this?	A car.
What are these?	Cars.
What's this?	A train.
What are these?	Trains.

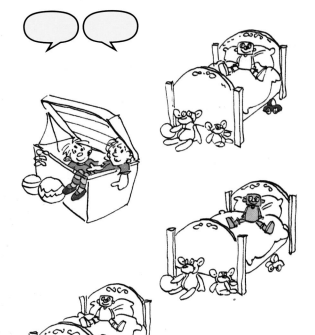

Where's the car?	Under the bed.
Where are the dolls?	In the toy box.
Where's the robot?	On the bed.
Where are the teddies?	By the bed.

Wake Up!

How many toys are there?

There's a kite on the chair.
There are three trains under the table.

The Toy Cupboard

BILL

SUZY

GARY

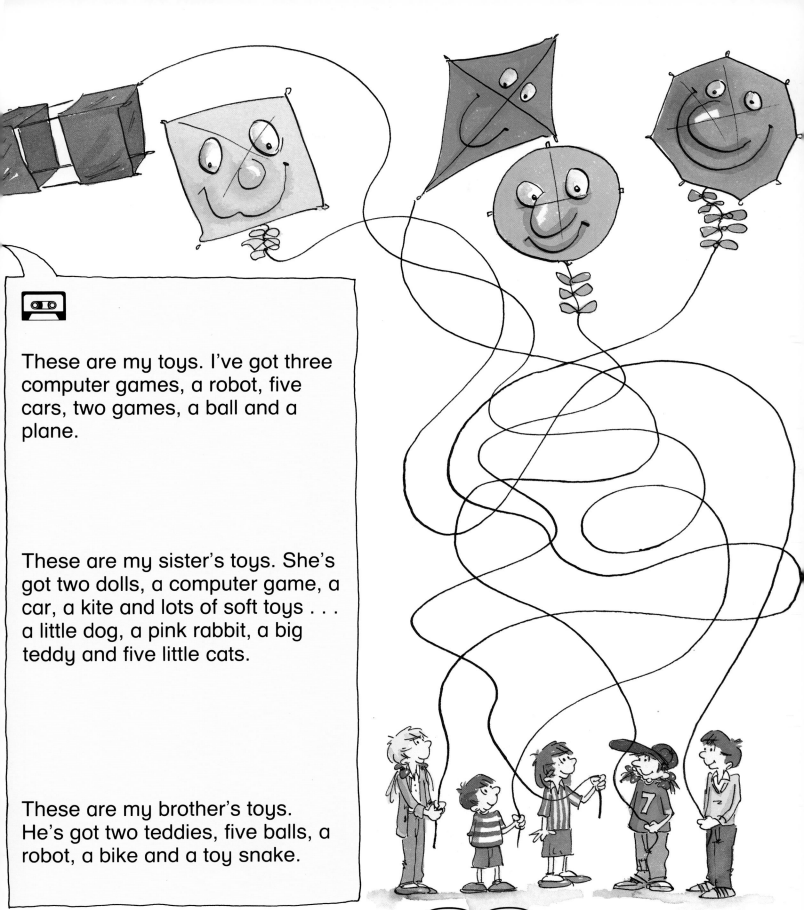

These are my toys. I've got three computer games, a robot, five cars, two games, a ball and a plane.

These are my sister's toys. She's got two dolls, a computer game, a car, a kite and lots of soft toys . . . a little dog, a pink rabbit, a big teddy and five little cats.

These are my brother's toys. He's got two teddies, five balls, a robot, a bike and a toy snake.

What colour are their kites?

A Red Tortoise!

 **RHYME**

18

1.
Jelly on a plate
Jelly on a plate
Wibble, wobble, wibble wobble
Jelly on a plate.

2. Teddy bear, teddy bear, turn around.
Teddy bear, teddy bear, touch the ground.
Teddy bear, teddy bear, tie your shoe.
Teddy bear, teddy bear, goodbye to you.

Paper on the floor,
Paper on the floor,
Pick it up, pick it up
Paper on the floor.

Suzy
Kay
My favourite
toy is my
computer game.
It is called
Pac Man.

Kate Brown
My favourite
toys are my cars.
They are yellow,
blue and
red.

The Toy Shop Game

STEPPING STONES GAME

SUPERSNAKE

Willy and Wendy are flying their kites. The little worm is Wendy's brother. He's called Wem. Wem is crying.

"Hello, Wem," says Supersnake. "Why are you crying?" "Because I haven't got a kite," says Wem.

"Now I've got a kite. My favourite snake," says Wem.

Hall of Mirrors

What colour is Julie's hair?   Blonde.

What colour are Julie's eyes?   Green.

How tall is Suzy?   1 metre 26 cm.

How tall is Kev?   1 metre 34 cm.

Look at Julie in the mirror.

Is Julie small?   Yes.

Is Julie's hair long?   No, it's short.

Is Julie thin?   No, she's fat.

43

Faces and Monsters

S O N G

Head and Shoulders . . .

Head and shoulders, knees and toes,
Knees and toes.
Head and shoulders, knees and toes,
Knees and toes.
And eyes and ears and mouth
and nose.
Head and shoulders, knees and toes,
Knees and toes.

Make a face   **You need:**   ⟵6cm⟶ ↕2cm ×7 card   a pencil   coloured pencils

2 Draw two noses:
one big nose
one small nose

1 Draw the eyes:
green eyes
blue eyes
brown eyes

3 Draw two mouths:
one big mouth
one small mouth

4 Make a face

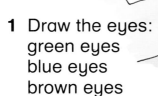

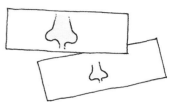
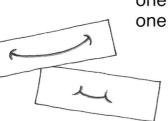

This is the Monster family. Mother and father are called
Zag and Zug. They've got three children, Zig, Zog, and little Zeg.

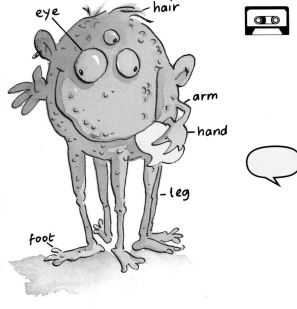

eye — hair
arm
hand
leg
foot

Zig is a big pink monster. His big
eyes are green and his little eye is
blue. He's got two hands but only
one arm. He's got five long legs and
five feet. His hair is purple.

Is Zig small?	No, he's big.
How many eyes has Zig got?	Three.
How many legs has Zig got?	Five.
What colour is his hair?	Purple.

45

Jack and the Giant

The Kay family are going to the cinema.

Who's the tallest?	Mr Kay.
Who's the smallest?	Gary.
Who's the tallest? Bill, Suzy or Mrs Mills?	Mrs Mills.
Who's the smallest? Mr Kay or Mrs Kay?	Mrs Kay.

The film is called "Jack and the Giant". It is Gary's favourite film. This is a picture of Jack and the Giant. The Giant is very, very tall and Jack is standing on his hand.

Who's got the biggest hands?	The Giant.
Who's got the shortest legs?	Jack.
Who's got the biggest teeth?	The Giant.

Measure your hands and feet

You need: 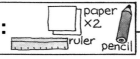 paper ×2, ruler, pencil

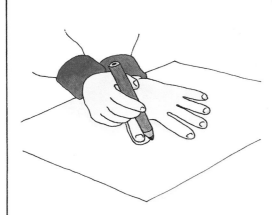  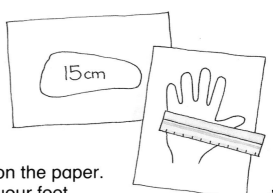

15cm

1 Put your hand on the paper.
2 Draw around your hand.

3 Put your foot on the paper.
4 Draw around your foot.
5 Measure your drawings.

How big are your hands and feet?

 Our Class

Who's got the shortest hair?

Who's got the biggest feet?

Who's the smallest?

Who's the tallest?

Who's got the smallest hands?

Who's got the smallest feet?

Who's got the biggest hands?

Who's got the longest hair?

 Kev's Family

This is me and my family. I've got brown hair and blue eyes. My sister Kate has got brown hair and brown eyes. My mother and father have got black hair and blue eyes. My father is the tallest in the family.

Kev Brown

Little Red Worm

1

2

3

4

5

Is it a man?	*No.*
Is it a woman?	*Yes.*
Has she got blonde hair?	*Yes.*
It's picture 5.	

6

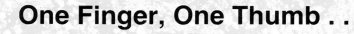

SONG

One Finger, One Thumb . .

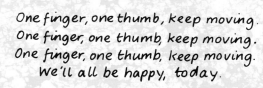

One finger, one thumb, keep moving.
One finger, one thumb, keep moving.
One finger, one thumb, keep moving.
We'll all be happy, today.

One finger, one thumb, one arm, one leg,
keep moving...

One finger, one thumb, one arm, one leg,
one nod of the head,
keep moving...

One finger, one thumb, one arm, one leg,
one nod of the head, stand up, sit down,
keep moving...

STEPPING STONES GAME

SUPERSNAKE

Hello, Little Red Worm. What's that?

A basket for my grandmother.

Let's go! Quickly!

Over there. There's my grandma's house.

Aha! A rat. Can I borrow your hat Little Red Worm.

Hello, grandma.

What a big nose you've got!

What big teeth you've got!

You aren't a worm. You're a rat!

And I'm not a worm.

Aaagh! It's Supersnake!

Thank you, Supersnake

Clothes

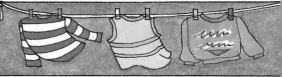

Getting Dressed

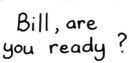

Bill, are you ready?

What are you doing?

I'm getting dressed.

Where are my yellow shoes?

They're under the bed.

Come on, hurry up Bill!

Where's my yellow jacket?

It's in the wardrobe.

What are you wearing?

My yellow jumper, jacket, trousers and shoes.

You look like a banana!

Where's Bill?	In his bedroom.
What's he doing?	Getting dressed.
What's he wearing?	A yellow jumper, yellow jacket, yellow trousers and yellow shoes.

Suzy, Bill and Gary are ready for school. Bill is wearing his yellow clothes. Suzy is wearing a t-shirt, a skirt, socks and shoes. Gary is wearing a t-shirt, shorts, socks and shoes.

Bye, mum.

Is Suzy wearing shorts?	No, she's wearing a skirt.
What colour is Gary's t-shirt?	Blue and white.
Are Suzy's socks red or white?	White.
What colour are Bill's clothes?	Yellow.

What number is on the sweatshirt?

- 1 a skirt
- 2 trousers
- 3 shorts
- 4 a jumper
- 5
- 6 a t-shirt
- 7 a jacket
- 8 socks

| 1 | Whose is this? | It's Suzy's. |
| 2 | Whose are these? | They're Bill's. |

R H Y M E Diddle, Diddle, Dumpling

Diddle, diddle, dumpling, my son John,
Went to bed with his trousers on.
One shoe off and one shoe on,
Diddle, diddle, dumpling, my son John.

Is Kate wearing her t-shirt?	No, she isn't.
What's she wearing?	A dress.
What colour is it?	Purple.
What's Kev wearing?	A shirt and tie.
Are Kev and Kate happy?	No, they aren't.

What a Mess!

It's cold today. The children are playing in the snow. Bill and Kate are making a snowman. He's wearing a black hat and a scarf. Kate is wearing a big cardigan and boots. Bill is wearing a coat and a red hat.

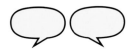

What colour are Bill's boots?	Green.
What colour is Kate's cardigan?	Purple.
Is Kate wearing a coat?	No, she's wearing a cardigan.
What colour is Bill's coat?	Blue.

What's he wearing?

Who is the spy?

Mr. Black ☐   Mr White ☐   Mr Grey ☐   Mr Green ☐

Oh no! The artist has put the wrong clothes on the children!

 **Point to Bill.**

Whose t-shirt is this?	Gary's.
Whose trousers are these?	Kev's.
Whose shoes are these?	Gary's.

Is he tall? Yes, he is.
Is he wearing brown shoes? Yes, he is.
Is he wearing a red tie? No, he isn't.
It's Mr White.

SUPERSNAKE

What are these?

They look like trousers. But whose are they?

Snail, are these your trousers?
No, I haven't got any legs.

Centipede, are these your trousers?
Don't be silly! I've got a hundred legs.

They look like Fly's trousers.
Thanks, Centipede.

Fly, are these your trousers?
How many legs have they got?

Eight.
I've only got six legs. They're Spider's trousers. She's got eight legs.

Here are your trousers Spider. Come on Fly. Let's go!

Round-Up Unit

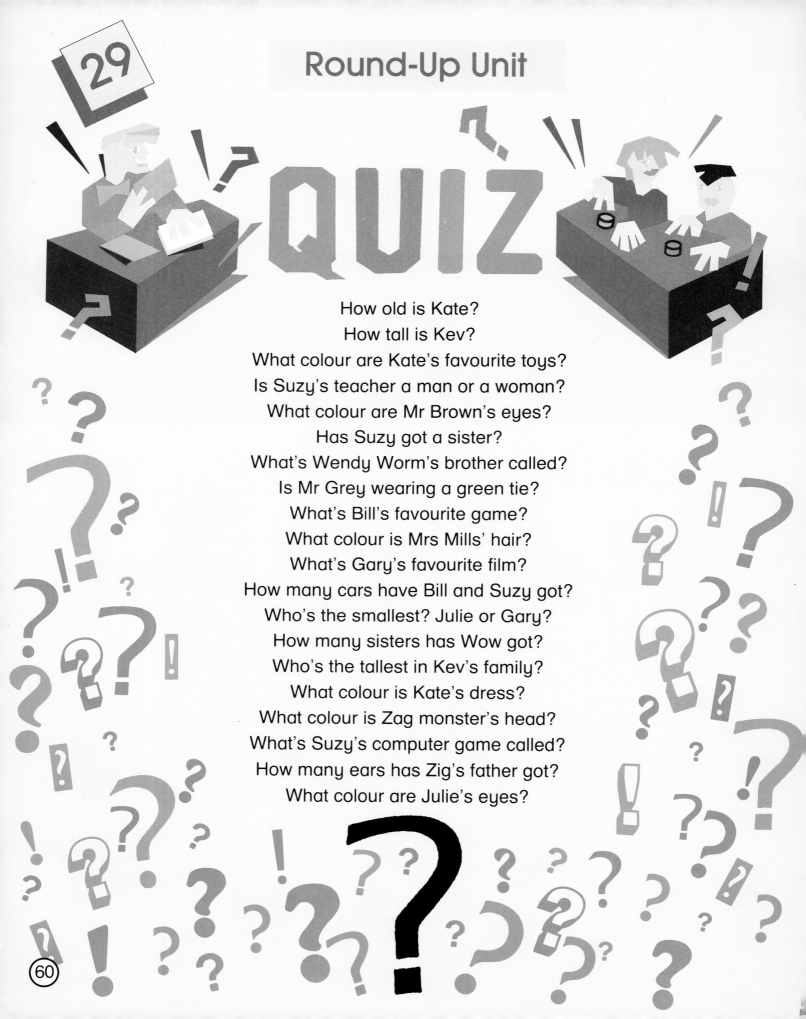

QUIZ

How old is Kate?

How tall is Kev?

What colour are Kate's favourite toys?

Is Suzy's teacher a man or a woman?

What colour are Mr Brown's eyes?

Has Suzy got a sister?

What's Wendy Worm's brother called?

Is Mr Grey wearing a green tie?

What's Bill's favourite game?

What colour is Mrs Mills' hair?

What's Gary's favourite film?

How many cars have Bill and Suzy got?

Who's the smallest? Julie or Gary?

How many sisters has Wow got?

Who's the tallest in Kev's family?

What colour is Kate's dress?

What colour is Zag monster's head?

What's Suzy's computer game called?

How many ears has Zig's father got?

What colour are Julie's eyes?

This is Bill's letter to his penfriend, Tom.

Dear Tom, My name is Bill Kay. I'm nine years old. I'm 1 metre 35 tall. I've got black hair and blue eyes. I've got one brother and one sister. My brother is called Gary. He's five. My sister is called Suzy. She's eight. I've got a tortoise called Slow. Slow is thirteen years old.
My favourite colour is yellow and my favourite game is scrabble.
your friend,
Bill

SUPERSNAKE

Why are you crying Wem?

Because I've finished my book.

It's O.K. Don't cry. Here's Book Two!

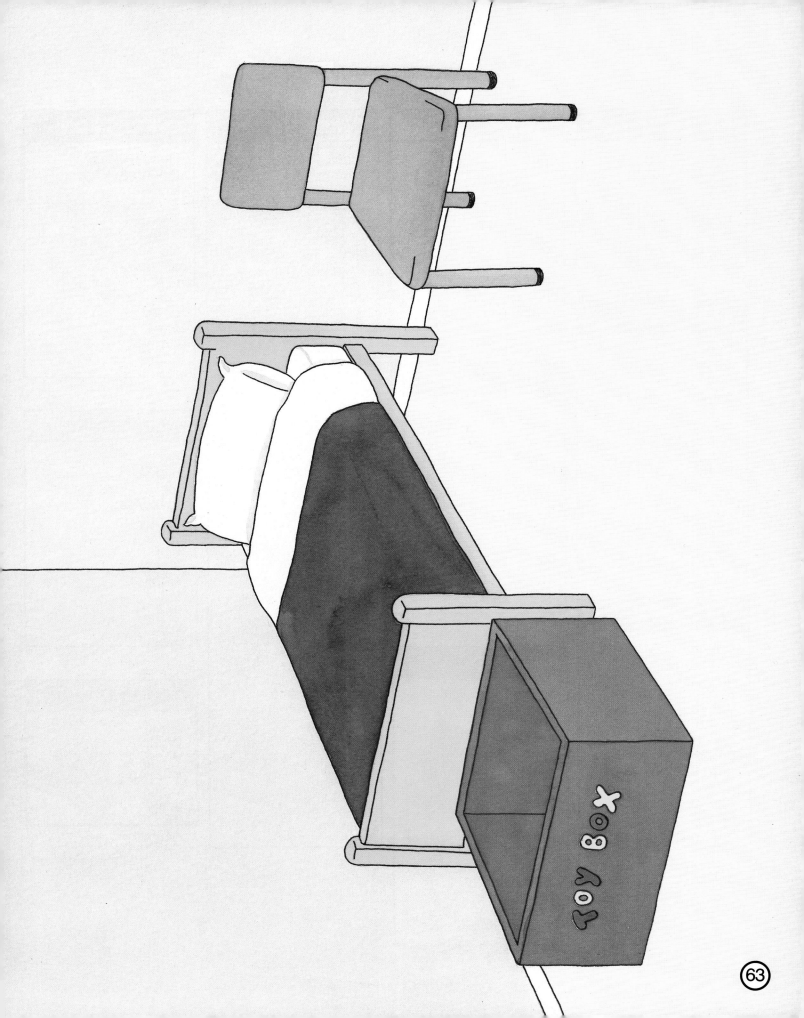

WORD GROUPS

PETS

- bird
- cat
- dog
- mouse
- rabbit
- snake
- tortoise

CLASSROOM

- bag
- book
- box
- chair
- door
- pen
- pencil
- pencil-case
- picture
- rubber
- ruler
- sharpener
- table
- teacher

PEOPLE

- boy
- brother
- children
- family
- father
- friend
- girl
- grandfather
- grandmother
- man
- mother
- Mr
- Mrs
- sister
- woman

TOYS

- ball
- bike
- car
- computer
- doll
- game
- kite
- plane
- robot
- teddy
- train

THE BODY

- arm
- ear
- eye
- finger
- foot (feet)
- hair
- hand
- head
- leg
- mouth
- nose
- toe
- tooth (teeth)

CLOTHES

- boots
- cardigan
- coat
- dress
- hat
- jacket
- jumper
- shirt
- shoes
- shorts
- skirt
- socks
- sweatshirt
- tie
- trousers
- T shirt

COLOURS

- black
- blue
- brown
- green
- grey
- orange
- pink
- purple
- red
- white
- yellow

NUMBERS

- one
- two
- three
- four
- five
- six
- seven
- eight
- nine
- ten
- eleven
- twelve
- thirteen
- fourteen
- fifteen
- sixteen
- seventeen
- eighteen
- nineteen
- twenty
- thirty
- forty
- fifty
- sixty
- seventy
- eighty
- ninety
- hundred

EXPRESSIONS

- Hello (Hi!)
- Goodbye (Bye!)
- Please
- Thank you (Thanks)
- Sorry
- Yes
- No
- of course
- O.K.
- I don't know
- Look!
- right
- wrong
- guess

ADJECTIVES

- big
- blonde
- fat
- favourite
- happy
- little
- long
- short
- small
- tall
- thin
- very

QUESTIONS

- How?
- What?
- Where?
- Who?
- Whose?
- Why?